W9-BFT-212

Illustrated by: Michael Denman

educate • nurture • inspire
www.warnerpress.org

God Creates the World

Long ago, there was no world at all. Everything was dark and still.
But even then God was there, and He had a plan.

What did God say? Cross out every V.
Then write the letters you have left in order on the blanks.

START
▽

⎯ ⎯ ⎯ ⎯ ⎯ ⎯ ⎯ ⎯

⎯ ⎯ ⎯ ⎯ ⎯ ⎯ ⎯ ⎯ ⎯ ⎯ **!**

Here are some things God made.
Can you match the pictures that go together?

God looked at everything He had made.
"This is good!" He said. Then God rested.

Find these things hidden in the picture:
apple, snake, cross, flower, and Bible

When Jesus Was a Boy

When Jesus was 12, Mary and Joseph took Him to Jerusalem.
What were they going to celebrate?

Write the first letter of each picture in the boxes to find out.

When it was time to go home, Mary and Joseph left with their group. They thought Jesus was with them. Soon they found out He was lost!

Help Mary and Joseph go back to Jerusalem.

START

Mary and Joseph looked everywhere.
Where did they find Jesus?

Connect the dots.

Cain and Abel

Cain and Abel were brothers.
When God liked Abel's offering best, Cain was so angry he killed Abel.

Put an X on 5 things that do not belong in the picture.

...ain's sin kept him away from God. God does not want anger to control us. When you feel angry, what can you do to feel better?

Draw a line between the words and pictures that match.

Pray

Walk

Talk

Write

Draw

John the Baptist

John the Baptist was not like other people.
He wore camel's hair clothes and ate locusts and wild honey.

How many locusts can you find in the picture? _____

John the Baptist preached in the desert.
He said someone special was coming soon.
Who was it?

Follow the lines from the sandals to the boxes they touch.
Write the letters to read the word.

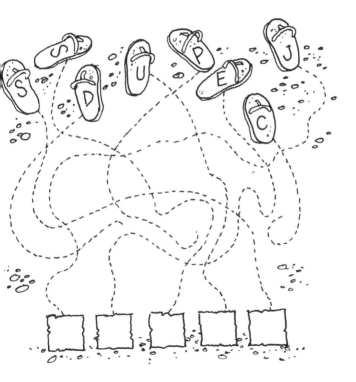

Noah's Ark

God told Noah, "Build an ark.
Then take your family and the animals inside."

Why did God want Noah to do this?
Write the letter on the line that comes AFTER the letter under the line.

G O D W A S
— — — — A —
F N C V   R

S E N D I N G A
— — — — — — — A
R D M C H M F

F L O O D T O
— — — — — — —
E K N N C S N

C O V E R T H E
— — — — — — —
B N U D Q S D

E A R T H
— A — — —
D   Q S G

ABCDEFGHIJKLMNOPQRST
UVWXYZ

When the ark was ready and everyone was inside,
the rain came pouring down.

How long did it rain?
Color in the spaces with dots to read the answer.

The Tower of Babel

"Let's build a city, so we can all live close together," said God's people.
Brick by brick, they began building a VERY tall tower.

Put an X on 5 things that do not belong in the picture.

When God saw the tower, He was not happy.

What did God do? Use the code to read the answer.

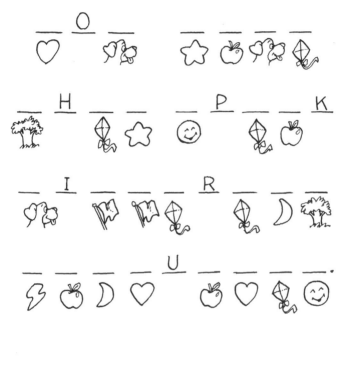

GOD MADE

THEM SPEAK

DIFFERENT

LANGUAGES.

G = ♡ D = 🐕 M = ☆ N = 🌙 E = 🪁
T = 🌳 F = 🚩 A = 🍎 S = ☺ L = ⚡

Fishers of Men

When Jesus was walking beside the Sea of Galilee, He saw two brothers.

What were they doing?
Find the letters **F**-**I**-**S**-**H**-**I**-**N**-**G** hidden in the picture.

"Come, follow Me!" Jesus said.
Right away, the men left their nets and went with Jesus.

Find and circle two fish that are exactly the same.

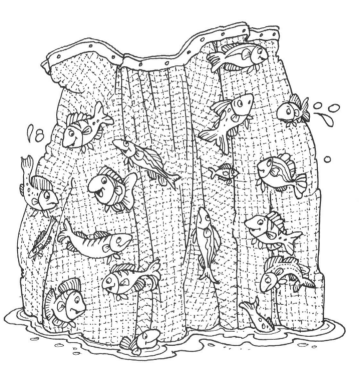

Jesus told the brothers they would have a new job from now on.

What would they be? Trace the lines from the fish to the blank lines.
Then write the letters to read the answer.

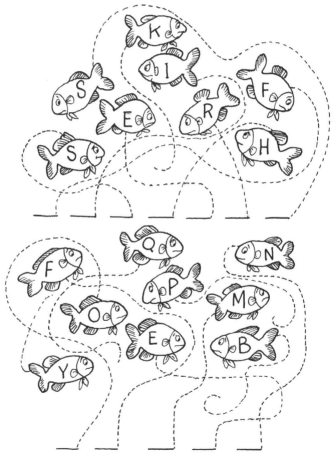

A Son for Abraham

Abraham and Sarah had no children. Now they were very old.
Sarah believed she would never be a mother.

Find and circle these things in the picture:
baby bottle, teddy bear, pacifier, spoon, and Bible

But God said they would have a son, and God's words came true!
Abraham and Sarah named their son, Isaac.

What does the name Isaac mean?
Color in the spaces with dots to read the answer.

The Wedding Miracle

Jesus, His mother Mary and the disciples were at a wedding.
Then Mary hurried to Jesus.

What did she say? Cross out every Z.
Then write the rest of the letters in order on the lines.

_ _ _ _ _ _ _ _ _

_ _ _ _ _

_ _ _ _ .

Jesus told the servants to take some water to the man in charge of the party. When he tasted it, the water had changed.

What was it? Trace the lines from the jars to the boxes they touch. Then write the letters to read the answer.

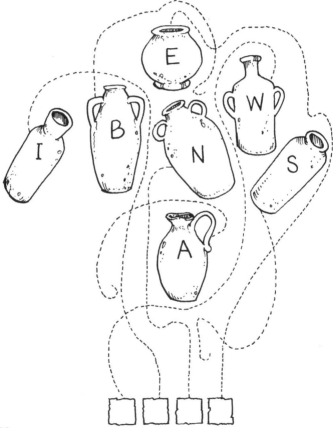

Turning <u>water</u> into <u>wine</u> was <u>Jesus'</u> first miracle. A <u>miracle</u>
is an <u>amazing</u> thing that happens only with <u>God's</u> help.

Find and circle the <u>underlined</u> words in the puzzle below.

```
G J E S U R J M G S
W A T J E S U S O F
I T H O S P M W D I
N A U B T R D A P Z
E A M A Z I N G T O
R Q A S T V B N G U
D M L M W A T E R O
T C O Z D I M I V H
G I M I R A C L E P
```

Jacob and Esau

Isaac and Rebekah had twin sons. Isaac loved Esau best.
Esau had red hair and was big and strong. He liked to hunt.

Draw a line between the pictures that match.

Jacob was Rebekah's favorite son.
He liked to stay home and was a good cook.
One day Esau came home from hunting. He was VERY hungry.

What was Jacob cooking? Connect the dots.

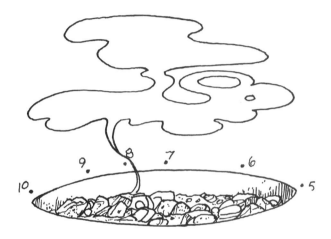

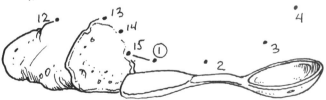

A Gift for Joseph

Jacob had 12 sons. He loved one of them more than all the others.

Who did Jacob love most?
Write the first letter of each picture in the boxes to find out.

Jacob gave Joseph a beautiful coat. The brothers were so jealous they sold Joseph to travelers. They tore up the coat and told Jacob they didn't know where Joseph was.

Find these things hidden in the picture:
lion, money, gift, heart, and Bible

The Woman at the Well

Jesus sat down by a well to rest. Soon a woman came to draw water.

What did Jesus ask her? Cross out every Z.
Then write the rest of the letters on the lines to read the answer.

__ __ __ __ __ __ __
__ __ __ __ __ __ ?

Jesus knew everything the woman had ever done.
She knew Jesus must be someone special.
She ran to tell everyone about Jesus.

What did she ask? Use the code to find out.

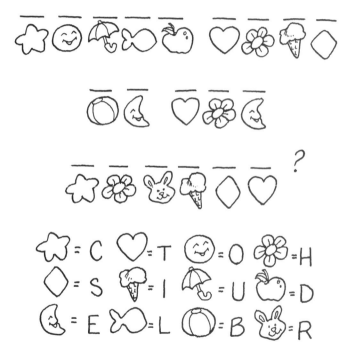

Jesus stayed for two days and taught the people.

Who did they believe He was? Color the spaces with dots to find out.

A Baby in a Basket

Pharaoh wanted to kill all the baby boys.
One mother would not obey. She hid her baby until he got too big.

Then what did she do? Write the words in the shapes that match.

She ____ a ____ and ____ her

____ in it.

baby

made

basket

put

The mother put her baby in the river. Soon, Pharaoh's daughter came and heard the baby crying. She picked him up gently.

Put an X on 5 things that do not belong in the picture.

Pharaoh's daughter said, "This baby will be my son now."
When he was old enough, she took him to the palace.

What did Pharaoh's daughter name the baby?
Write the first letter of each picture on the lines to find out.

Jesus Heals a Crippled Man

One day Jesus saw a crippled man who had waited
by the healing pool for 38 years. Jesus asked him a question.

What was it? Write each letter that comes
AFTER the letter under the line to find out.

$\overline{}\ \overline{}\quad \overline{}\ \overline{}\ \overline{}$
C N   X N T

$\overline{}\ \overset{A}{\overline{}}\quad \overline{}\ \overline{}\quad \overline{}\ \overline{}\ \overline{}\ \overline{}$
V A   M S   S N A D

$\overline{}\ \overline{}\ \overset{A}{\overline{}}\quad \overline{}\ \overline{}\ \overline{}\ ?$
G D A   K D C ?

ABCDEFGHIJKLMNOPQRST
UVWXYZ

"Get up! Pick up your mat and walk," Jesus said.
The crippled man's legs became strong. Jesus had made him well!

Find these 5 things hidden in the picture:
cane, bandage, glasses, spoon, and Bible

The Burning Bush

One day Moses led his sheep to green grass near Mount Horeb.

Help Moses and the sheep go to the mountain.

Suddenly, Moses saw something strange!

What was it? Write the words in the shapes that match to find out.

A _____ WAS ON _____

BUT DIDN'T _____ UP.

BURN

BUSH

FIRE

Then <u>Moses</u> heard something <u>strange</u>!
A <u>voice</u> from the <u>bush</u> called his <u>name</u>.
The voice was <u>God</u>! He had a <u>special</u> <u>job</u> for Moses to do.

Find and circle the <u>underlined</u> words.

```
R U B U J S T N G Z
J V O I C E U S Q P
I Q H O S P N P R I
S P E C I A L J O B
M E M A N A D O N T
O L B U S H F F R U
S X G O D A V B M I
E C O H S L W N E E
S S T R A N G E H F
```

Four Men Tear Up a Roof

Four men took their friend to Jesus to be healed.
But there were so many people that they couldn't get close to Jesus.

What did they do? Use the code to find out.
The first one has been done for you.

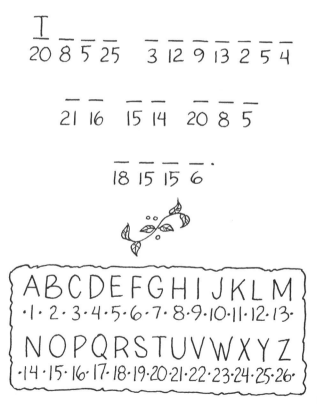

T _ _ _   _ _ _ _ _ _ _
20 8 5 25   3 12 9 13 2 5 4

_ _   _ _   _ _ _
21 16   15 14   20 8 5

_ _ _ _ .
18 15 15 6

A B C D E F G H I J K L M
·1· 2· 3· 4· 5· 6· 7· 8· 9· 10· 11· 12· 13·

N O P Q R S T U V W X Y Z
·14· 15· 16· 17· 18· 19· 20· 21· 22· 23· 24· 25· 26·

The men dug a hole through the roof.
Then they lowered their friend down to Jesus.
When Jesus saw how much they believed, He healed their friend.

Find these letters hidden in the picture: **H-E-A-L-E-D**

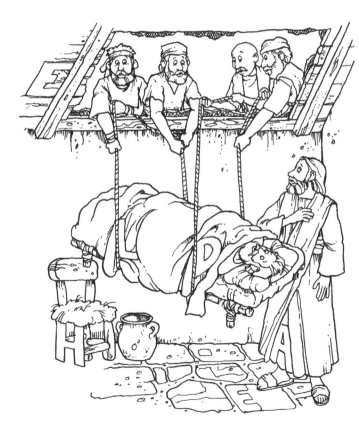

The 10 Commandments

God said, "I am making some laws for My people.
The laws will help them obey Me."

What were the laws called? Cross out every K.
Then write the letters you did not cross out on the lines.

___ ___ ___ ___ ___ ___ ___ ___

___ ___ ___ ___ ___ ___ ___ ___ ___

Moses listened carefully to what God said.
Later, he told the people what God wanted them to do.

Put an X on 5 things that do not belong in the picture.

The Story of the Sower

One day a farmer was planting seed.
Some fell on the path and birds ate it.

How many birds do you see? _____

But some seed fell in good soil.
The plants grew well and produced a good crop.

What did the farmer grow? Finish the picture.

The Battle of Jericho

God wanted Joshua to capture the city of Jericho.
He told Joshua what to do.

What did God say? Use the code to find out.

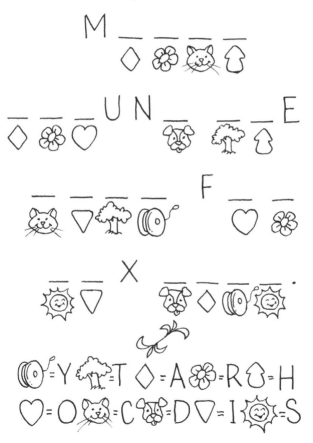

M _ _ _ _ (◇ ❀ 🐱 ⬆)

_ _ _ U N _ _ _ E (◇ ❀ ♡) (🐶) (🌳 ⬆)

_ _ _ _ F _ _ (🐱 ▽ 🌳 ◎) (♡ ❀)

_ _ X _ _ _ _ _ . (☀ ▽) (🐶 ◇ ◎ ☀)

◎ = Y   🌳 = T   ◇ = A   ❀ = R   ⬆ = H

♡ = O   🐱 = C   🐶 = D   ▽ = I   ☀ = S

Write the words in the shapes that match.

On the seventh day, the people

marched  times, the

blew and

then the people gave a loud

.

priests

shout

seven

trumpets

46

Jesus Calms the Storm

Jesus and His disciples were on a boat when a terrible storm came.
Water was coming into the boat. The disciples were afraid!

Where was Jesus? Cross out every Z and Q.
Then write the letters you have left on the lines to read the answer.

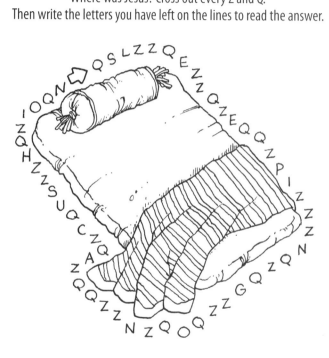

__ __ __ __ __ __

__ __ __

__ __ __ __ __

Jesus woke up. He told the storm to be still.
Right away, the wind and waves calmed down.

What did the disciples say? Look at the numbers on the shapes.
Then write the words in the shapes on the lines where they belong.

___ is ___ ?
  1   2

Even the ___ and ___
          3   4

___ ___ !
 5   6